GEO·GAMI

CREATE MULTIDIMENSIONAL GEOMETRIC ORIGAMI

BY KATHERINE A. GLEASON

ILLUSTRATED BY MERYL HENDERSON • ORIGAMI PAPER DESIGNED BY ATIF TOOR

STERLING INNOVATION
New York

Before you start making a figure,
check that you have enough sheets
of origami paper in the required
pattern to complete the figure.

STERLING INNOVATION
New York

An Imprint of Sterling Publishing
387 Park Avenue South
New York, NY 10016

© 2006 Metro Books.

Designed by Atif Toor.
10 9 8   ISBN 978-0-7607-7225-6   Manufactured in China

HEXAHEDRON

A hexahedron is a solid figure with six faces. The word comes from the Greek terms *hex*, meaning "six," and *hedron* or *edron*, meaning "base" or "seat." In the realm of Platonic solids, the hexahedron is composed of identical square sides. In common parlance, a Platonic hexahedron is known as a cube. This irregular hexahedron is made up of six right triangles. You will need three sheets of origami paper to complete this figure.

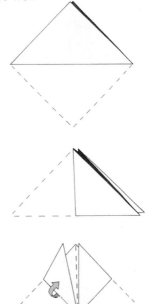

 Fold the paper in half on the diagonal and crease well. Fold the triangle in half by bringing the left point over to meet the right. Crease well and unfold. Bring the left and the right points up to meet the top point and crease well.

2 Make two more modules in the same way. Hold one module in your left hand with the open points pointing up. Hold a second module in your right hand with the open points pointing to the left. Slide the points on the right-hand module into the triangular pocket in the left-hand module.

3 Hold the third module so the open points point to the right. Slide the module down onto the open points of the left-hand module.

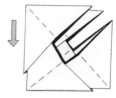

4 Tuck the open points on the third module into the pockets of the right-hand module. Cently press the figure together. You may have to rotate the figure and squeeze, rotate and squeeze some more to get the modules flush.

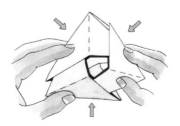

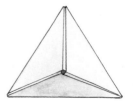

Once completed, these figures form half a stellated octahedron and a whole stellated octahedron. An octahedron is an eight-sided figure. When stellated, the faces of the figure are extended to make starlike points. You will need 12 sheets of origami paper to make the first figure, 24 sheets to make the second figure, and some glue.

 1 Following the directions on pages 4–5, make four Hexahedrons.

 2 Working on a flat surface, arrange the four Hexahedrons so they nestle together. Dab a little glue on the inside surfaces and press the pieces together.

HEXAHEDRONS TOGETHER II

1 Following the directions on pages 4–5, make eight Hexahedrons.

2 Working on a flat surface, glue four Hexahedrons together as you did on page 6. Glue the remaining four Hexahedrons together in the same way. Once the glue is dry, glue the flat bottoms of the Hexahedron groupings together.

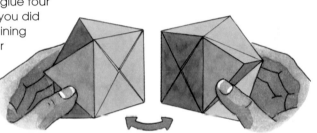

M. C. Escher, the famous graphic artist, was fascinated by tessellation, the practice of filling a space with repeating, interlocking designs. Origami artist Nick Robinson created a version of this arrow figure. You will need four sheets of paper to complete this project, which is constructed from four modules.

 With the color you want your figure to be facedown, fold the paper on the diagonal, crease well, and unfold. Fold the paper on the other diagonal, crease well, and unfold. Fold the bottom right corner to meet the center point and crease well. Do the same thing to the bottom left corner.

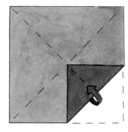

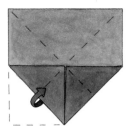

2 Unfold the two corners. Then refold so that the points meet the crease mark. Then lift the blunted corner and refold on the existing crease.

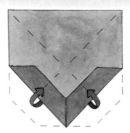

3 Fold the top edge down to meet the module's center line, crease well, and unfold. Fold the top edge down to meet the crease you just made.

4 Fold the right corner down so the flap's bottom edge meets the module's center line. Do the same thing on the left side.

5 Turn the module over. Fold the bottom point up to meet the module's center. Fold the left point to meet the center. Fold the top edge down, reversing the existing crease. Crease all of these folds well.

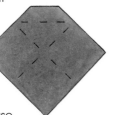 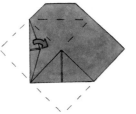 

6 Fold the right point in to meet the center and unfold. Refold the point so that it meets the crease you just made. Then refold the blunted point at the crease.

Complete Steps 1–6 with the three remaining sheets of paper. Making sure that they are oriented the same way, place two modules next to each other. Raise the left point on the right module and fold it over the blunted point of the left module. Crease well. Place the third module under the left module and attach it by wrapping the point in the same way. Attach the remaining module to the two adjacent ones. Turn the whole figure over, and your Tessellation is done.

The sun's corona, of course, is not really pointed, but this figure, which is made up of oblique triangles, does seem cheerful and sunny. To complete this model, you will need eight 3" x 3" sheets, so cut two pieces of origami paper into four equal squares.

1 Keeping the main pattern you want to see on the inside, fold the paper in half on the diagonal and crease well. Bring the top point down so the right side of the paper meets the bottom edge, crease well, and unfold. Bring the top point down again, this time so the left side of the paper meets the bottom edge. Crease well.

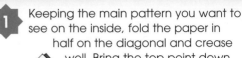

2 Unfold the last crease you made. Pull the edges of the top point toward each other, and pinch from the spot where the creases meet to the tip of the point. The point will stand up, and the edges of the flap will meet the module's bottom. Fold the small triangle down to the right.

3 Turn the module over. Raise the flap on the left and, leaving the small point down, fold it to the right. Crease well. Raise the point again and fold it back to the left so that it lies evenly between the module's two horns.

4 Turn the module over and make seven more. Begin to join the modules together by inserting the horn of one into the pocket of the other.

5 Fold the small central point up to secure the horn in the pocket. Keep adding modules one by one. Add the eighth one to complete the circle and your Pointed Corona is done.

FLUTED DIAMOND

This figure was developed by Molly Kahn, daughter of Lillian Oppenheimer, the founder of the Origami Society of America. Viewed from one pointed end, this figure displays eight flaps, which make up a star. To complete this figure, you will need two sheets of origami paper.

 Keeping the pattern you want on the outside, fold one sheet of paper in half on the diagonal. With the long side of the triangle held away from you, fold in half again so that the left point meets the right point.

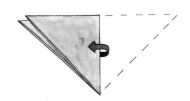

2 Lift the top triangle and fold it back over itself. Unfold the crease you have just made. Put your fingers inside the top triangle, open it, and flatten it along the creases so that it forms a square.

3 Turn the paper over. Fold the top right flap down to meet the bottom point. Unfold the crease you have just made. Put your fingers inside the flap, open it, and flatten it as you did in Step 2. You have now completed the Preliminary Base.

Make sure that the open ends of the paper are pointing down. Fold the top layer of both sides in so that the upper edges meet the center crease. You will now have an upside-down kite shape. Turn the paper over and do the same on the other side.

Unfold the right flap. Gently lift and open it. Flatten the flap. Move the flattened right flap out of the way and open the left flap. Flatten it, too. Turn the whole figure over. Unfold and flatten both the right and left flaps as you did before.

Make a second module, identical to the first. Open up both modules. Insert the points of each figure into the pockets of the other. This may take longer than you think, but have patience. With a bit of squeezing and wiggling, the two modules will merge into one figure.

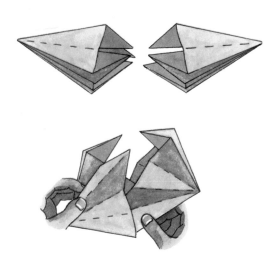

SKELETAL OCTAHEDRON

A regular octahedron has eight faces, each of which is an equilateral triangle. A skeletal octahedron forms the inner framework for these eight sides. You will need six sheets of origami paper to make this figure. For a nice effect, use two sheets each of three different colors.

Keeping the color you want on the outside, fold one paper in half on the diagonal, crease well, and unfold. Fold the paper in half on the other diagonal, crease well, and unfold.

2 Turn the paper over. Fold it in half by bringing the bottom edge up to meet the top edge. Crease well and unfold.

 3 Turn the paper over again. Hold the edge of the paper at the center crease. Pull the edges in toward the center and down, so that the paper bends at the existing creases and the edges come to rest on top of one another. You have just completed the Water Bomb Base.

 4 Raise the points on the right and fold them over to the left. Crease well and unfold.

Repeat Steps 1–4 with the remaining five sheets of paper. If you are using three different colors, select two modules of different colors. Hold Color Number One in your left hand and Color Number Two in your right. Open up the modules and position them so you have two arms of each module vertical and two horizontal. Tilt the Color Number Two module and slide its lower point inside the lower point of the Color Number One module.

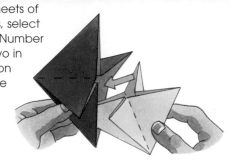

 Select a module made from your third color. Slide one of its horizontal arms down over a horizontal arm of the Color Number One module. Slide the lower vertical arm of the Color Number Three module inside the closest horizontal arm of the Color Number Two module.

 Select the other module of Color Number One. Place one arm inside an empty arm of the Color Number Three module. Slide the lower arm down over the arm of Color Number Two.

8 Select the other module of Color Number Two. Place two opposite arms inside the arms of the Color Number One modules. Place the arm between them down over the arm of the Color Number Three module.

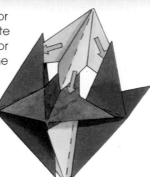

9 Add the final module by sliding two opposite arms down over the arms of the Color Number One modules. Insert the other two arms inside the arms of the Color Number Two modules and squeeze the modules together.

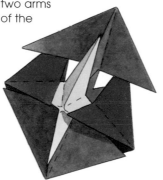

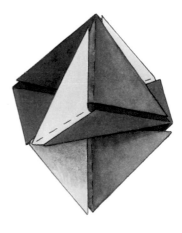

STELLATED OCTAGON

If you like, think of this figure as an eight-pointed star. An octagon, of course, is a two-dimensional shape with eight sides. And a stellated octagon has had its edges extended to form starlike points. You will need one sheet of origami paper, a pair of scissors, and a little glue.

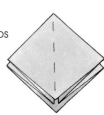

 1 Complete the Preliminary Base by following Steps 1–3 of Fluted Diamond, pages 14–15.

2 Check that the open ends of the paper are closest to you. Fold the top layer so that the bottom edges meet the center crease and you have a kite shape. Crease well.

3 Bring the top point down and crease well. Unfold the crease you have just made and the creases you made in Step 2.

4 Grasp the bottom point. Raise it up and away from you. The paper will bend at the crease you made in Step 3. Press the edges in to meet in the center as you flatten the figure. You will end up with a long diamond shape. Turn the figure over.

 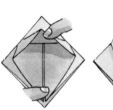 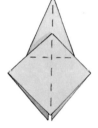

5 Complete Steps 2–4 on this side. Note that the bottom half of the diamond is split in two.

  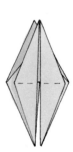

6 Rotate the figure 180 degrees so that the split bottom point is at the top.

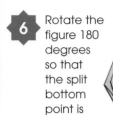

7 Grasp one long point of the lower half of the figure in each hand. Gently separate your hands so that the small triangle in the center flattens into a square and the two pyramidal flaps point up.

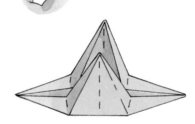

8 Starting with the front pyramidal flap, pinch the sides together so the edges touch. Press the paper at the base down flat so that the small flap sticks straight up.

Holding the base of the small flap down, fold it over to the right so that the inner straight edges align. Then fold it down so that its straight edge makes a right angle with the bottom edge of the figure. Crease well.

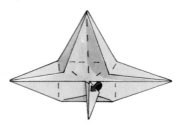

10 Unfold the small flap and lift it from its base. Put your finger inside the flap. Flatten the flap into a small kite shape by pushing the point down.

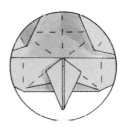

11 Rotate the figure so that the remaining pyramidal flap is facing you. Complete Steps 8–10 on this side.

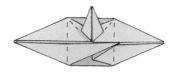
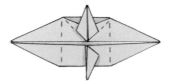
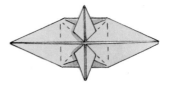

12 Fold the left flap to the right at the existing crease. Then, at the figure's vertical center line, crease the flap to the left. Do the corresponding thing with the right flap.

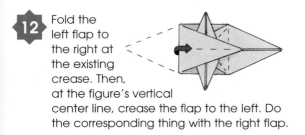 

13 Raise the inside corners of the left flap and fold them to meet the center line. Crease very well and do the same thing with the right flap.

 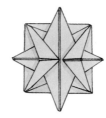

14 Open the folds you made in Step 13 and bend the paper backward along the creases so that the corners end up under the flaps.

 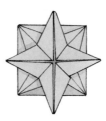

15 Turn the figure over. Carefully cut along the crease mark on the base from the figure's edge to the spot underneath where the sides of the flaps meet. Then fold the edges back to meet the diagonal creases. Do the same thing with the three remaining sides.

16 Dab a little glue under the flaps that you folded in Step 15. Turn the figure over, and you are done!

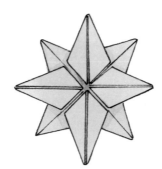

In its open, ringlike position, this figure takes the shape of an octagon. In its closed pinwheel position, it forms, well, a pinwheel. You will need two sheets of origami paper in two different colors. Cut each sheet into four smaller squares. You will make eight identical modules from these squares.

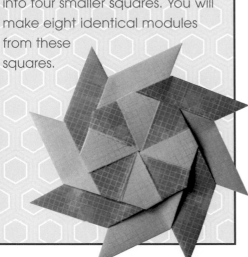

 Fold one square of paper in half by bringing the bottom edge up to meet the top edge. Crease well and unfold. Bring both corners on the right in to meet the center line. Crease well. Fold the module in half by bringing the top edge down to meet the bottom edge.

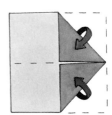

2 Fold the top left corner down to meet the bottom right corner, crease well, and unfold. Fold the top left corner back behind the figure along the crease you just made. Crease well.

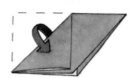

3 Unfold the corner from behind the figure and open the layers slightly. Using the existing creases, tuck the corner inside the module.

4 Make seven more modules by following Steps 1–3. To start combining the modules, make sure the open points of the first module are pointing to the left. Place the closed end of the second module between the first module's open points. The open points of the second module should be pointing down. Fold the tips of the first module's open points inside the layers of the second module, leaving a hairbreadth of space between the fold and the edge of the second module. Slide the second module down, as shown.

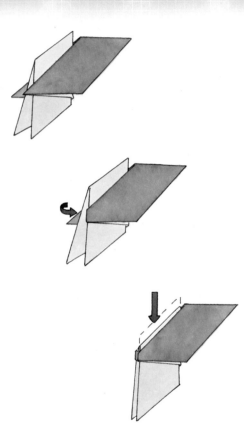

5

Add a third module in the same way. Keep adding modules until you reach the last one. Then join the two ends together by folding the tips of the last module inside the first module.

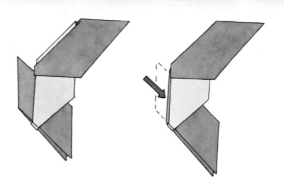

To transform your ring into a pinwheel, push gently on opposite sides. Rotate the figure and push some more. Keep rotating and pushing until the modules all meet in the center.

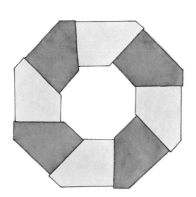

If you consider the planes formed by the openings as faces, this figure has ten sides —eight paper trapezoids and two square openings. And decahedron means just that —a solid shape with ten faces. This figure is made of four modular units, so you will need four sheets of origami paper.

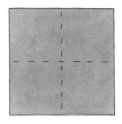

 With the color you want for your module facing up, fold the paper in half by bringing the bottom edge up to meet the top edge, crease well, and unfold. Fold the paper in half the other way and unfold. Fold all four corners to meet at the center and crease well.

2 Turn the module over. Raise the bottom corner, allowing the flap underneath to pop out and crease so that the edge meets the centerline.

3 Do the analogous thing with the top corner.

4 Raise the lower right inner corner. Allow the flap underneath to pop out as you do this and crease so that the right edge meets the center line. Do the analogous thing with the top left inner corner.

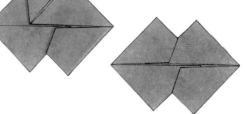

5 Turn the figure over. Fold the figure in half by bringing the left point over to meet the right point.

6 Fold the top point back over to the left so that it meets the left edge and crease. Turn the figure over and do the analogous thing on the other side.

7 Raise the top layer of the bottom point. Crease it on the diagonal, following the line of the flap just beneath it. Tuck the point into the pocket. Fold the top flap down in the same way, crease well, and unfold.

8 Turn the figure over. Fold the top flap down, crease, and tuck it into the pocket. Fold the bottom point up, crease well, and unfold. Lift the top layer on the right and unfold the module.

9 Make three more modules by following steps 1–8. Turn each module over and crease along the center line by bringing the left side over to meet the right. Open the fold you just made. To create your Irregular Decahedron, slide the tabs of each module into the pocket of another and press the modules together gently.

 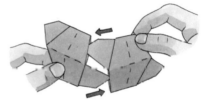

A dodecahedron has twelve faces. This figure has ten paper trapezoid-shaped faces and two pentagonal openings, which count as additional sides. It's made of five modules, so you'll need five sheets of origami paper.

1 Make five modules by following Steps 1-8 of Irregular Decahedron with Square Openings, pages 32–35.

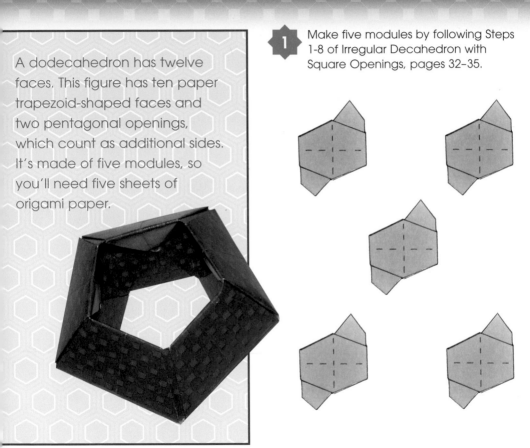

2
Turn each module over and crease along the center line. Open the fold and slide the tabs of each module into the pocket of another. Press the modules gently together to form the figure.

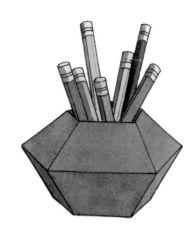

IRREGULAR HEXADECAHEDRON

A hexadecahedron is a solid shape with sixteen faces. Hexadecahedron is a pretty unusual word. Typically, such a figure would be called a sixteen-faced solid, but the Greek-rooted term does have a nice ring to it. This hexadecahedron has twelve trapezoidal faces and four triangular openings. You can also think of this figure as a truncated, stellated pyramid. To make it, you will need six sheets of origami paper.

 Make six modules by following Steps 1–8 of Irregular Decahedron with Square Openings, pages 32–35.

 Allowing the modules to bend at the existing center crease, join three of them together. They will form one of the triangular openings.

3 Add a fourth module on the right side.

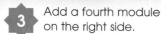

4 Add a fifth module on the far side. Pull this fifth module down and insert its tab in the pocket of the fourth module. This will form the second triangular opening.

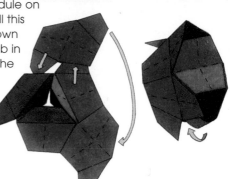

5 Attach the sixth module to form two more triangular openings. Gently squeeze all the modules together.

Designer Lewis Simon created this model, which he calls a Gyroscope, although it does not spin exactly like its namesake. This model is best made with twelve smaller squares of paper. Select three sheets of origami paper in three different colors. Cut each sheet into four smaller squares.

 1 Select two squares of each color and fold module one, the Water Bomb Base, by following Steps 1–3 of Skeletal Octahedron, pages 18–19.

2 Fold the remaining six squares into Preliminary Bases by following Steps 1–3 of Fluted Diamond, pages 14–15.

3 Open up one Preliminary Base and one Water Bomb Base. With the colors you want facing down, place the Water Bomb Base on top of the Preliminary Base. Line up the creases as shown on both sheets. Fold the edges on the Preliminary Base in so that they wrap around the edges of the Water Bomb Base. Leave a hairbreadth of space between the fold and the edge of the paper.

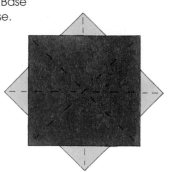
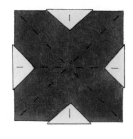

4 Push the sides of the figure in again the way you did when you made the Water Bomb Base. Combine the remaining modules in the same way.

Slide one tab of one combined module over the tab of another and inside the outer layer, as shown.

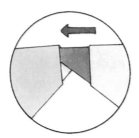

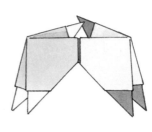

6 Attach a third combined module first to one module of your original pair and then to the other. Note that the combined modules will no longer lie flat.

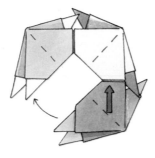

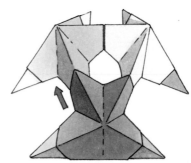

7 Attach the remaining combined modules so that each one lies opposite its color pair.

Note: Hold the completed figure loosely between your palms, blow on it, and it will spin.

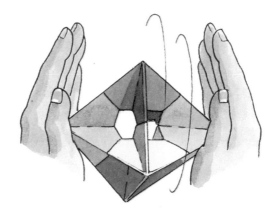

X-FACED CUBE

The cube is the most commonly found regular geometric solid. Also known as a Platonic hexahedron, it is one of five Platonic solids, which include tetrahedrons, octahedrons, icosahedrons, and dodecahedrons. You will need six sheets of origami paper to complete this modular figure.

 1 Fold a sheet of origami paper in half by bringing the bottom edge up to meet the top edge. Crease well and unfold. Fold the top and bottom edges in to meet the center line and crease well.

 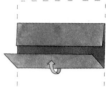

2 Turn the figure over. Fold the top left corner down to meet the center of the bottom edge. Make sure that the folded edge on the underside of the figure gets folded, too. Fold the bottom right corner up to meet the top edge in the same way.

3 Fold the lower left point up to meet the module's top point. Fold the upper right point down to meet the module's bottom point. Crease well, unfold, and turn the module over. Make five more modules exactly like this one.

4 Make sure all the modules have their slit side facing up. Combine three modules by placing the points of two modules inside the opening on the face of a third.

5 Keep adding modules, bending as needed, to tuck in the loose points and create your X-Faced Cube.

STAR CUBE

A six-sided solid with starlike projections? That's a stellated hexahedron! First you will need six sheets of origami paper to make an X-Faced Cube. Then you will need an additional six pieces of origami paper to construct modular star attachments for each face of the cube.

 1 Make one X-Faced Cube, pages 44–45. With the color you want for your modules facedown, fold the paper in half by bringing the left side to meet the right. Crease well and unfold. Fold the paper in half the other way by bringing the bottom edge up to meet the top edge. Crease well and unfold. Fold both edges in to meet the center line.

 2 Fold the right and left ends in to meet the center line. Then fold each inner corner to meet the meet the module's edge at the center line.

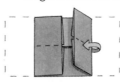

3 From the top of the figure, grasp the top layer of the inner corner of the triangle on the right. Pull it out and crease the paper on the underside so that the point lies flat. Do the same thing to the remaining three points.

4 Fold the entire module on the diagonal by bringing the top right corner down to meet the bottom left corner. Crease well and unfold. Fold on the other diagonal by bringing the top left corner down to the right. Crease well and unfold.

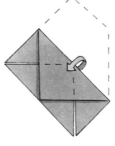

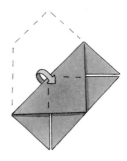

5 At the module's center crease, squeeze the sides of the module toward the center. Allow the top points to come down to meet the bottom points. Flatten the module.

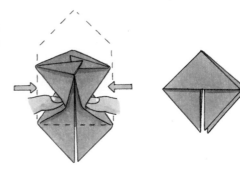

6 Raise the lower right point and fold to meet the module's top point. Crease well. Turn the triangular flap at the top right to the left as if you were turning the page of a book. Raise the remaining lower right flap, fold to meet the top point, and crease well.

7 Turn the module over. Raise the lower right point, fold to meet the top point, and crease well. Turn the triangular flap to the left as you did in Step 6. Raise the remaining point, fold, and crease.

8 Allow the module to open and become three-dimensional. Tuck each lower triangular flap into a slit on the face of your cube. Complete five more star modules and attach them to the cube, as well.

  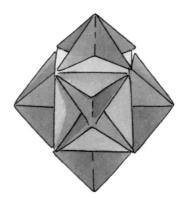

BURSTING STAR CUBE

Make the X-Faced Cube, pages 44–45, then make six star modules by following the steps for the Star Cube, pages 46–49. Before you attach the star modules to the cube, modify them by following the steps on these two pages.

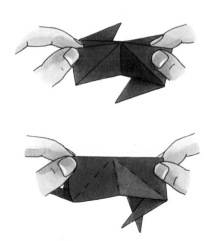

 Hold the star module at one of the center lines and pinch to reverse the center crease so that instead of sinking, it rises toward you. Rotate the module 90 degrees and do the same thing to the other center crease.

2 Reverse both the diagonal creases.

3 Modify the remaining five modules and attach all six to your X-Faced Cube.

CUBE OCTAHEDRON

Known as a quasi-regular solid, the cube octahedron is made up of six square faces and eight triangular faces. You can think of it as a combination of a cube and a regular octahedron. Or imagine it as a truncated cube, in other words, a cube with its corners sliced off. This model was designed by Tomoko Fuse, the Japanese master and reigning queen of modular origami. You will need three sheets of origami paper to complete this figure. Before you begin folding, cut each sheet in half to form six rectangles.

 1 Fold the bottom left corner up to meet the center of the top edge. Crease well. Fold the top right corner down to meet the center of the bottom edge. Crease well.

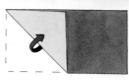

2 Fold the top right point down to meet the lower point and crease well. Fold the lower right point up to meet the top point.

Lift the loose lower left point and crease the flap in half by bringing the point up to meet the top point. Do the analogous thing with the loose upper right point. Turn the module over. Complete five more modules in the same way.

 Looked at from the front, each module should have a flap that projects down from the upper left corner of the square. Insert the left point of one module into the right pocket of another module.

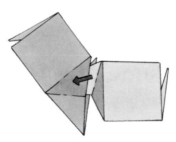

Add another module to create an inverted pyramid.

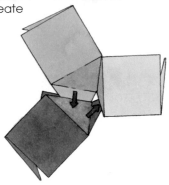

 Add a fourth module to create an open triangle bounded on two sides by your first and third modules.

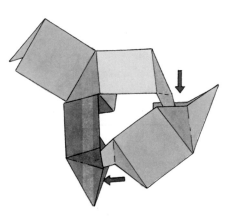

7 Add the fifth module to create a second inverted pyramid.

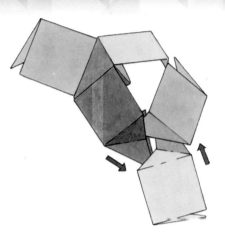

8 Add the final unit and your Cube Octahedron is done.

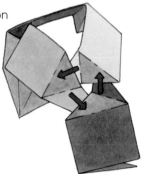

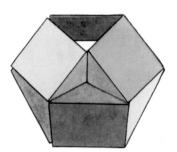

It's another regular hexahedron! This one is constructed from six modular units that take the shape of parallelograms. You will need six sheets of origami paper. Select three different colors for this figure and use two sheets of each.

 1 With the color you want facedown, fold the paper in half by bringing the bottom edge up to meet the top edge. Crease well and unfold. Bring the top and bottom edges in to meet the center line. Crease well and unfold. Fold the top left corner and the bottom right corner to meet the creases you just made, leaving a hairbreadth of space between the short edge and the crease.

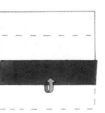

2 Fold the blunted corners so the folded edge comes toward the crease. Leaving just a hairbreadth of space between the edge and the crease will make the next fold easier to execute. Fold the top and bottom sections in toward the center line at the existing creases.

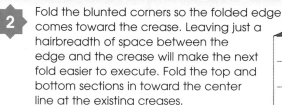 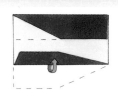

3 Lift the bottom left corner and crease so that the corner meets the middle of the top edge. Do the analogous thing to the top right corner and you will have a parallelogram.

4 Open the figure slightly and tuck the left flap inside so it lies underneath the diagonal edge that slopes down from left to right. Tuck in the right flap in the same way.

5 Raise the left point and fold the figure in half along the vertical center line. Crease well. Then fold the point down to the left so it comes to rest on top of the lower left corner. Crease well.

Turn the figure over so that the triangle's right angle is on the right. Fold the lower left point up to meet the top point. Crease well. Allow the module to open up into a parallelogram with a creased surface. Make five more parallelogram modules for a total of six.

Select one module. Its color will be Color Number One. Pick a second module to be Color Number Two. From the lower edge, insert the tip of the Color Number Two module into the left pocket of the Color Number One module. Then, from the right side, slide the tip of a Color Number Three module into the lower pocket on your Number Two module.

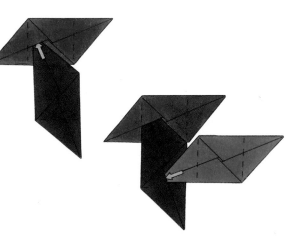

8 Add the second Color Number Two module by placing its tip in the remaining pocket of the Color Number One module. Add the second Color Number Three module by inserting its point into the remaining pocket on your first Color Number Two module. Allow the developing figure to fold along the existing creases and tuck the points of the Color Number one module into the adjacent Color Number Three modules.

9 Add the final module by inserting the tips into the empty pockets on the two Color Number Three modules.

For this figure, you will use the modular parallelogram module that you made for the Woven Cube. You will need 12 sheets of origami paper in four different colors. As you did when making the Woven Cube, you will assign numbers to each color to help you keep track of the modules. In this case, you may want to write down each color next to its number assignment.

 1 Select one module of each color and weave them together by inserting one tip of each module into the pocket of another. The developing figure will become three-dimensional. Make sure that the central point where all the modules meet rises toward you.

2 Add a second module of each color. Keep in mind that each individual module only hosts one other color. So, if a Color Number One module has one pocket occupied by a Color Number Two tip, the second pocket will also host a Color Number Two tip. Tuck the loose points from the first group of modules into the pockets of the second group.

3 Add a third module of each color while keeping the pattern of the colors consistent. Tuck in the loose points and your figure is done.

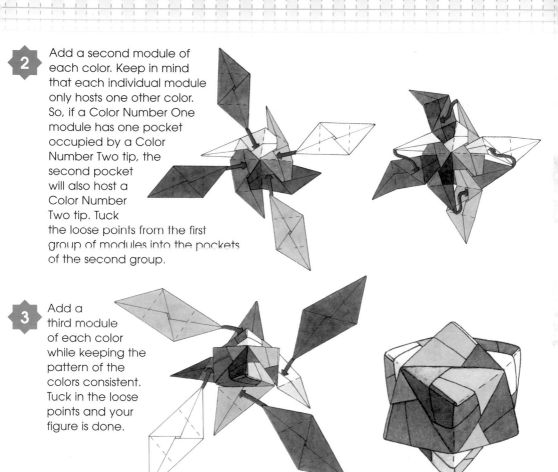

DODECAHEDRON

A regular dodecahedron is a Platonic solid with twelve sides, each of which is a pentagon. Platonic polyhedra (many-sided three-dimensional shapes) are also called perfect or Pythagorean solids. To make this figure, you will need 12 sheets of origami paper. Because the figure is made on a rectangle, you will also need scissors, a cutting blade, or a paper cutter.

 1 Trim each sheet so that it measures 6" x 4 1/2". Fold the paper in half so that the bottom edge meets the top edge. Crease well and unfold. Fold the left edge over to meet the right. Crease well and unfold.

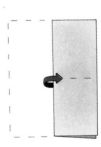

2 Fold the top left corner down to meet the center point. Fold the lower right corner up to meet the center point. Crease both these folds well. Then fold the top right corner down to meet the center point. Fold the lower left corner up to meet the center point. Crease both folds well.

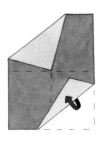

3 Fold the module in half by bringing the lower point up to meet the top. Crease well. Open the figure slightly and slide the two inner tabs to interlock.

4 Fold the left arm of the figure so that its upper corner meets the center line. Make sure that the top edge of this flap is parallel to the bottom of the module. Fold the left arm in the same way.

5 Unfold the two flaps that you folded in Step 4. Make 11 more modules. Turn them over so that their arms are pointing away from you. Combine three modules together into a section, as shown. Combine the remaining modules into sections in the same way.

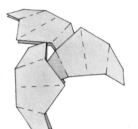

6 Combine three of the sections together. Then add the one remaining section.

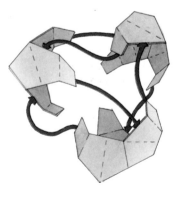